Synthetic and Practical Manual of the Tarot

Eudes Picard

Synthetic and Practical Manual of the Tarot

— Major and Minor Arcana
— Interpretation

Eudes Picard

SYNTHETIC AND PRACTICAL MANUAL OF THE TAROT
© and translation 2022 by Daniel Bernardo

ANTIQUA SAPIENTIA

https://antiquasapientia.publiebook.com

Translated from:

Manuel Synthétique et Pratique du Tarot

ISBN: 978-1-989586-80-8

Table of Contents

Preface

The treatises on the Tarot that have been published to date have contributed to the curiosity of the occultist public. These treatises, compiled – for the most part – with a sense of profound respect for the Tradition, present, however, very different characters in their conception, adaptation and method. Thus, the adept may experience certain doubts when choosing the best work, the safest, the most definitive one. After all, all works are good when they are inspired by tradition. But it is necessary to liberate the essential part of it; this is the objective we intend to achieve by presenting this *Synthetic and Practical Manual of the Tarot*.

This Manual consists of two main divisions: the explanation of the cards and their manipulation. In the explanation of the cards, we have clearly distinguished the Major Arcana from the Minor Arcana, and summarized, in the form of a compilation, the opinions of the modern masters on the 22 Major Arcana of the Tarot. Each card is copied from the Tarot de Marseille, the best in our opinion. The drawings have no other purpose than to reproduce in broad strokes each arcanum as a whole. The details of the attributes whose precise and profound meaning makes the value of the symbols so evident have been scrupulously respected. Much work remains to be done, especially the addition of the colors which are the indispensable complement to the planetary and zodiacal correspondences. In our reproduction, the reader will be able, first of all, to distinguish the Tarot de Marseille from other more fantastic or extravagant Tarot decks. This is the essential point.

The study devoted to the fifty-six Minor Arcana is original. The plan on which it is based will be developed at length.

The designs are executed according to magical and kabbalistic traditions. However, one will be surprised at the choice of certain symbols. The explanation of this will be made clear. The author has tried above all to represent very clear arcana which immediately awaken an absolute and complete sense. The Manual ends with the method of interpretation. This will be its practical side. The most commonly used procedures are recalled. Some references, which our experience allows us to recommend, have been added.

E.P.

The Tarot

What is the Tarot?

The Tarot is a deck of cards, but it is a deck that cannot be played with. It instructs, it does not distract, and its object is to reveal the future. However, this is not its particular character. Considered from a higher point of view, it summarizes the system of the Universe; it reveals to us the world of Ideas and Principles, it enables us to grasp certain laws of the evolution of phenomena. For this very reason, the Tarot constitutes one of the most marvelous methods of divination.

However, to analyze a phenomenon, it is not enough to recognize it. It is necessary to trace its origin, to know its cause, to follow its development. The Tarot provides us with these mysterious coordinations that link, by deduction, the cause with the effect.

At first sight, the Tarot surprises us. The weirdness of its symbols, its naive scheme and even the dryness of its images impress us. It is said of the Tarot that it is very strange. One can smile but not laugh. Surprise suppresses criticism. One does not understand anything at first, but instinctively feels that one is before a monument, and then one begins to wonder if, behind such arcana, with their crude appearance, there is something more than a work of the imagination. As one examines this extraordinary book more closely, the mystery becomes clearer. The paper becomes a mirror in which the functions of numbers, colors and symbols are reflected. Little by little, everything is harmonized, classified in spirit, clarified; in a word, one begins to decipher the multiple meanings of the cards. The operation requires a firm will, a profound knowledge of occultism, a marked affinity with the outer world and, in our opinion, above all this, a rare intensity in the faculties of meditation supported by science and method.[1] This point of view is essential and presides over the most rational system of Tarot manipulation. It is therefore good to insist on the exercise of conscious meditation on condition that one does not lose oneself in it.

Meditating on a pentagram means examining it in its smallest details and striving to unravel its meanings without ever straying from the general sense. The aim of this meditation is to stimulate the intuition without losing it. Therefore, one will not possess the science of the Tarot if one is not erudite and intuitive.

* * *

The history of the Tarot is confusing. Many versions circulate about its genesis. Not being able to rely on texts or monuments, one has to accept the different opinions that mark its great stages through different races and through time. In reality, it is not known exactly where it came from. It is unlikely that any human genius was complete enough to compose it. The ideas it contains are universal and immutable. They go back to the earliest needs of observers tormented by the desire to grasp, through form, numbers and symbols, genial visions of the universal mechanism. The Tarot would thus be a collective work, sketched by ancient seers and consecrated by a mysterious tradition.

Like the Iliad, the Tarot has its chanters, who have transmitted to us, without commentary, a kind of celestial epic. A characteristic sign of the Tarot, and which specifies the definitive part of its conception, is shown in the fact that, through the centuries, its background has not changed much. We find a similar scheme in most of the different ancient and modern Tarot decks.

The modifications concern the details of the form and betray the imagination of the artists. To convince oneself of the reality of these

---

1   We recommend reading the works of Court de Gébelin, Jacques Gaffarel, Guillaume Postel, Stanislas de Guaita, Oswald Wirth, Paul Christian, Papus, J. G. Bourgeat, R. Falconnier, and especially the work of Éliphas Lévi: *Dogme et rituel de la haute magie.*

observations, it is sufficient to examine the collection of Tarot decks in the National Library.[2]

Consequently, it can be said of the Tarot that it has been transmitted to us rather modified than deformed; and leaving aside purely historical research, it is full of clarity in the domain of esotericism. That is why we must pay all our attention and direct our research to its esoteric and symbolic part.

Let us not forget that the ancients, faithful to the magical ritual, boasted silence about its mysteries. Only the initiate participated in the cultural ceremonial and knew the revealed Truth. Nothing has changed. The truth is always within our reach. It is necessary to discover it, to go towards it and to try to possess it through the methodical degrees of initiation.

We think it is useful to remember first of all to approach the study of the Tarot with great simplicity, without cluttering the spirit with a multitude of complicated terms or points of view.

We recommend a well-understood occult education that leaves the spirit with clear notions. The study of the Kabbalah is necessary; also a knowledge of astrology will be of the utmost importance in learning the planetary and zodiacal correspondences. Assuming, therefore, that the adept is prepared, let us take a Tarot. When unfolding its 78 cards, we will immediately notice that 22 of them are distinguished from the other 56 by characteristics that recall a general idea or characterize an individuality.

Once this first distinction has been established, we have before our eyes two series of arcana that form, so to speak, two Tarots. The first 22 cards are called Major Arcana and the other 56 are called Minor Arcana.

Originally, the Tarot was composed only of the 22 cards comprising the Major Arcana. The incorporation of the other 56 cards, from which our present deck of cards is derived, apparently dates back to the Middle Ages. Their introduction is said to be due to the Gypsies, who are said to have handed them down to us. This is an important point, since such a hypothesis would tend to suggest that the 56 minor arcana predate Charles VI, and that rather than having been created spontaneously for the amusement of a king, they had been in existence for a long time. Let us say this in order to rehabilitate the 56 minor cards which are much

---

2   The author refers to the *Bibliothèque nationale de France* (Translator Note).

neglected and generally considered to be foreign to the Tarot. Later we will see how these cards form the logical continuation of the major cards. For the moment we can say that the Tarot comprises 78 cards and not 22; but that the nature of the two groups is different and that they constitute two great planes: an upper or celestial plane, represented by the 22 Major Arcana, and a lower or terrestrial plane, represented by the 56 Minor Arcana. Each of these planes completes itself. They are intimately linked and correspond in the same proportions as effect to cause or absolute to relative.[3]

---

3   This book was published in 1909; today we know the history of the Tarot a little better, and the most serious scholars agree that the Tarot appeared in Italy in the 15th century (late Middle Ages), and from there it spread to France and the rest of Europe. On the other hand, Picard makes it clear that his Manual concentrates on the symbolic and esoteric aspect of the Tarot, not on its history (TN).

Major Arcana - I

As a whole, the Major Arcana apply to the Absolute, to Causes, to Principles. They reflect the sidereal world, the planets, the zodiac, the numbers, the letters and the complete evolution of man. It could be admitted that it is in these 22 prototypes of the Principles that the divine Plato must have glimpsed the world of Ideas.

Each letter is presented under a triple aspect: the symbolic, the numerical or alphabetical and the astrological.

We will not dwell here on metaphysical considerations. The practical plan of this Manual obliges us to set aside abstractions in favor of the concrete.

The letters and numbers are inspired by the Kabbalah and find their correspondence in the Hebrew alphabet. The astrological relationships evoke the influences of the planets and the signs of the zodiac; finally, each card summarizes the idea or type it represents by the title of its symbol. It is important to keep the exact term of each card in its interpretation. This is the simplest and clearest way. Through meditation, one must delve into all the details, starting from the principle that each card contains an infinite number of nuances that are something like sub-symbols. These nuances accentuate its initial meaning and show us its greatness.

Let us take a random example: Card VI, entitled *The Lover*. It shows an adolescent between two women. The arcana evoke the myth of Hercules between Vice and Virtue. The young man hesitates. He does not know which of the two women he should follow. We observe his feet turned outwards, each one in an opposite direction; this is the first confirmation of the doubt in the choice of direction, applied to the motor organ par excellence. The soles of the feet are glued to the ground, so there is no movement, the adolescent seems riveted to the ground. His arms are invisible, as if, by showing them, the slightest gesture could betray a movement of his will. He turns his eyes to Vice, the only indication of attention on his part. He simply looks, without effort, without desire.

What a difference in the attitude of the women! Their feet are hidden. Her hands, on the other hand, act and seem to demand immediate determination. Vice, placed on the right, advances her right hand over the adolescent's organs of generation, as if to designate the seat of desire; Virtue, on the left, places her left hand over his heart, seat of feelings, while modestly lowering her right hand in protest at Vice's gesture.

Vice, with its bestial profile, looks defiantly at Virtue. In the sky, a Genie of a higher order, in the center of a heart-shaped Sun, directs an arrow at the heart of the young man. His gesture presages the victory of feelings. His heart is blue, the color of spirituality.

In short, the arcana indicate the struggle on equal terms between the passions and the feelings; by extension, they mark that time of indecision that precedes the moment when man chooses between good and evil. Could this duality be better summarized than in the traits of the *Lover*, that is, the man who is about to give in to the attraction of the senses?

This card is under the dominion of Virgo, an earth sign. In the interpretation, we will first stay with the meaning of the tradition: *The Lover*, taking care to compose the surrounding cards in order to assign it a definite meaning which must not deviate from the dominant idea of hesitation in the face of trial.

This is how the arcana should be examined. We will try to penetrate into their full meaning by all possible means. We insist on the necessity of analyzing the arcana one by one in numerical order. When one has assimilated the meaning of an isolated card, one will apply oneself to consider the 22 principal ones as a whole or in their perfect divisions.

Placed in two rows of 11 cards each, we will evoke the binary and by deduction, we will see that the upper row corresponds to the active cards and the lower to the passive ones. If we invoke the ternary, we will obtain 3 groups of 7 cards each corresponding to the three worlds: divine, moral and physical.

Considered as a whole, the Tarot represents the evolution of man. *The Magician* opens his cycle which closes in *The World*, taking man through the stages where he develops and perfects himself on all planes. *The Magician* has in front of him pentacles and swords. He holds a cup and a wand; this is the elemental quaternary by means of which man, supported by the will, will traverse the successive degrees of trials to the supreme goal of the Reward where he shines in the center of a crown. There he will have risen to the highest point of perfection. *The Magician* brings together the elements of matter; he coagulates it. The evolved man dissolves it, dismantles it, as it were, and casts it out of the circle of light where it reigns alone, armed with the scepter of power.

These quick descriptions give a general notion of the interpretation and combinations of the main cards. The care that must be taken in analyzing a card is obvious. No detail should be omitted. The example given for card VI, although incomplete, can serve as a model for the examination of all other cards.

In addition, the masters and scholars whose works we have mentioned will be the most valuable guides to consult on this subject.

Minor Arcana - I

The study of the Minor Arcana has never been developed. This harmony, this sequence that dominates the range of the 22 Major Arcana, is not perceived as a whole. The research plan lacks foundations. We do not perceive in the commentators of the Minor Arcana an affiliation of ideas. In fact, we do not know their key. It would be easy to adopt the meaning attributed to these cards without trying to find its reason. The serious adept demands more. For our part, we have tried to clarify the problem and, without claiming to solve it, we believe we have at least dealt with it in a way that may open new horizons to informed researchers. We have resorted to astrology according to the following principle: since the 22 Major Arcana represent the causes, the Minor Arcana must represent the effects. It is accepted that the causes are essential and belong to the system of the Universe. We will only perceive these causes if they manifest as effects that can be controlled by our senses and on a specific plane. This plane is the Earth. Thus, card VIII: *Justice*, represents not justice as we conceive it from the human point of view, but the model of Justice, the principle of Justice. To bend this universal attribution of the idea of Justice to the derived meaning we give it, we are obliged to descend to a lower and restricted plane. The major mode becomes minor. We then obtain a derived meaning that can be attributed to a fact or to an agent of human justice.

In summary, the card VIII evokes a universal idea of balance; while the swords will provide us with the complements of the principle of Justice, such as: judgments, crimes, sentences, magistrates, etc. The same happens with the other cards and their relationships.

This theory that assigns the causes to the celestial plane, and their effects, that is, the phenomena, to the terrestrial plane, is not the only one that tends to make us suppose that the Minor Arcana apply to the earthly plane.

We find other clues in their numerical scale, in the hierarchy of its figures, in the detail of its ornaments, in the division of the quaternary and the binary.

In fact, the 56 minor cards are divided into 4 suits of 14 cards each; each suit represents a symbol that goes in progression from 1 to 10 plus 4 cards that reproduce the human element considered from the social and hierarchical point of view. These 4 suits correspond to the 4 elements, namely: the cups to air, the scepters to fire, the swords to water and the pentacles to earth.[Here Picard departs from the usual assignment of the four elements to the four suits of the Tarot, assigning the cups to air and the swords to water, reversing the elements that most authors assign to these two suits (TN).]

If we examine the form of the symbols, we find that it is reduced to two expressions: the straight and the curve. Swords and scepters are straight and symbolize action, while pentacles and cups are circular and symbolize passivity.

We thus obtain 2 groups of 28 cards that evoke the idea of contrast and analogy of the binary.

The 4 cards with human figures further clarify the earthly relationships. They indicate age and social position. The Page will be the adolescent or subordinate; the Knight, a grown man; the Queen, a woman; and the King, a married man of advanced age.

Let us now look at the detail of the ornaments that adorn the cards. What do we see? Leaves, flowers and fruits.

It is certainly no coincidence that the artist has planted vegetation everywhere. He must have thought that the product that best testifies to earthly vitality is the plant. The choice of plants is also made with discernment.

The phases of growth: bud, leaf, flower, fruit are applied to the cards that signify the beginning, the evolution, the result and the consequences of a thing. Again, each card must be looked at very closely. However, a difficulty arises in distinguishing where the plant symbol ends and becomes an ornament. We have the feeling that, next to the symbol, fantasy sometimes takes primacy.

No matter. The first indication seemed to us so valuable that it served us as a guide for the realization of our drawings conceived with a more methodical sense and on which we owe the reader some explanations.

Each letter has two aspects: form and meaning.

The form is expressed through the drawing of symbols and elementary attributes. A geometrical plan has been adopted for the figures, reproducing certain magical pentacles whose fixed form harmonizes with the number and symbol of the card. Thus, each number evokes a correspondence of form that is proper to it and that is similar in the four suits. The number 6, for example, is expressed in the magic pentacles by two triangles forming a 6-pointed star. Thus, the 6 of cups, of swords, of scepters and of pentacles will be drawn by a 6-pointed star. The attributes that adorn the designs have no other purpose than to immediately recall the element of each symbol. Thus, the scepters will be in the fire, the swords in the aquatic element, the pentacles in the earth and surrounded by roots or young shoots, and the cups, of an aerial nature, will be decorated with flowers, butterflies or birds.

There is also a relationship of intensity between the strength of the card and the nature or quantity of the attributes. This pictorial correspondence of the elements has led us to make even more precise astrological comparisons of the periods of the year through the combined relationships of element, sign and month. Thus, the coarse, being of an igneous nature, correspond to the fire trine: Aries, Leo and Sagittarius, and are assigned the periods of March, August and November, months dominated by the influence of these 3 signs. The proportional part of the duration of the quarter (90 days), to be distributed among the whole group of 14 cards, gives a duration of influence of about 6 days for each card.

Below we summarize these correspondences in tabular form.

Scepters

Correspondence: Fire.

Signs: Aries, Leo, Sagittarius.

Months: March, July, November.

Correspondence of each card of the suit of Scepters with the periods of the year.

1	March 21 to 27
2	March 28th to April 2nd
3	April 3 to 8
4	April 9 to 14
5	April 15 to 20
6	July 21 to 27
7	July 28th to August 1st
8	August 2nd to 7th
9	August 8th to 14th
10	August 15 to 20
Page	November 21 to 28
Knight	November 29th to December 3rd
Queen	December 4 to 10
King	December 11 to 20

Pentacles

Correspondence: Earth.

Signs: Taurus, Virgo, Capricorn.

Months: April, August, December.

Correspondence of each card of the suit of Pentacles with the periods of the year.

1	April 21 to 27
2	April 28 to May 2
3	May 3 to May 8
4	May 9 to 14
5	May 15 to 20
6	August 21 to 27
7	August 28th to September 15th

8	September 2nd to 7th
9	September 8th to 14th
10	September 15 to 20
Page	December 21 to 28
Knight	December 28 to January 3
Queen	January 4 to 10
King	January 11 to 20

Cups

Correspondence: Air.

Signs: Gemini, Libra, Aquarius.

Months: May, September, January.

Correspondence of each card of the suit of Cups with the periods of the year.

1	May 21 to 27
2	May 28th to June 2nd
3	June 3 to 8
4	June 9 to 14
5	June 15 to 20
6	September 21 to 27
7	September 28th to October 1st
8	October 2nd to 7th
9	October 8th to 14th
10	October 15 to 20
Page	January 21 to 28
Knight	January 29th to February 3rd
Queen	February 4 to 10
King	February 11 to 20

Swords

Correspondence: Water.

Signs: Cancer, Scorpio, Pisces.

Months: January, October, February.

Correspondence of each card in the suit of Swords with the periods of the year.

1	June 21 to 27
2	June 28 to July 2
3	July 3 to 8
4	July 9 to 14
5	July 15 to 20
6	October 21 to 27
7	October 28th to November 1st
8	November 2nd to 7th
9	November 8th to 14th
10	November 15 to 20
Page	February 21 to 28
Knight	March 1 to 6
Queen	March 7 to 13
King	March 14 to 20

The objective value of these correspondences is very questionable. The fact that a date is associated with a card does not necessarily imply that the thing indicated by the card will take place on the date indicated. We must adopt a more general vision and stop, not on an isolated date, but on a period represented by all the cards of the same nature. If in a game the swords dominate, it can be logically deduced that the foreseen events will be able to come true in the periods ruled by the water signs. These are questions of skill that will be dealt with in the chapter on interpretation. We simply wanted to point out that the concordance of the months with the signs was logically given by the astrological correspondences.

We return to a question that has to do with the drawing of the Minor Arcana. There are figures and details that will seem strange. We have reproduced some animals whose presence in the middle of the arcana seems baroque, such as larvae, butterflies, birds and fish. The same is true of the Sun and the Moon, which are often used to emphasize a sense of activity or passivity. They are not signs represented as ornaments. They constitute a kind of punctuation of the idea of the arcana. We have sought, we repeat, to evoke in the eyes of the reader a translation as immediate as possible of the idea contained in the symbol.

The second aspect of each card is reserved for its meaning. After the form, the idea. This meaning seems to us to be twofold. It is quantitative and qualitative, that is, the letter has a numerical value and a qualitative value that determines its nature.

The quality provides the concrete and tangible side of the meaning. Thus, the pentacles will qualify money and nothing but money; the scepters, action; the cups, love; and the swords, resistance, struggle.

The numerical value provides a coefficient of intensity and fatality. The number is strong or weak; beneficial or bad. We have established relationships between the numerical meanings of the initial 10 Major Arcana and the initial 10 Minor Arcana of each group. In addition, we have maintained the kabbalistic value of each number. The note of fatality has been given to us by the beneficial or malefic character of the elements and the signs. The signs of fire and air will be considered beneficial and those of water and earth, malefic. The scepters and cups will be favorable, while the pentacles and swords are not. Thus, the beneficial and malefic symbols are opposed in pairs. In the same way the number can be considered in its good or bad relations, depending on whether it is applied to a beneficial or malefic symbol. The rule is complicated with too many nuances to be absolute; but it is advisable to keep it in mind in the main lines of interpretation. Let us analyze for example the number 6 in its kabbalistic and numerical value in relation to the Major Arcana:

Six is the number of Venus, of Beauty. Therefore, it is of a happy essence. In the Tarot, the 6 is *The Lover*, the card of trial, of indecision. In conjunction with the scepters and cups, the number 6 will be in harmony with the happy symbols; it will therefore have a beneficial meaning; it will be moral and physical beauty. The idea of beauty will prevail over that of hardship. On the contrary, in the 6 of pentacles and the 6 of swords, the bad side of the number appears first. It marks the times of stoppage, the problematic stages, the threats, without the beneficial aspect of the number being completely erased, and will be translated for the 6 of pentacles as lack of action, lack of decision about money, spirit of economy, fear of spending, greed; and for the 6 of swords it will manifest as a morbid state, that is to say the phase in which the organism is no longer in a state to fight for itself, where it is the plaything of two opposite forces: health and disease.

It follows from this explanation that if each card were to be analyzed in great detail, it would take several pages to comment on it. Moreover, the adept must draw clear and precise conclusions for himself, from his own meditations, from his own efforts, from the art of grasping the relations between the number and the symbol. We have tried to indicate the basis of the complex mechanism of the esoteric, astrological and symbolic elements. We hope that this summary will suffice to illuminate the obscure points of the minor cards and we now turn to their examination and interpretation.

Major Arcana - II

Card I - The Magician

A man standing. He has a youthful appearance; curly hair like Apollo or Mercury, a confident smile on his lips. He wears on his head a nimbus in the shape of ∞, a symbol of life and the universal spirit. He has before him swords, cups and pentacles; he holds a wand in his hand raised toward the sky, and a cup lowered toward his table in his other hand.

Astrological correspondence: The Sun.

Number: 1.

Letter: Alef א. (P.P.)[See the Bibliography, at the end of this Manual, to identify the references to the authors, shown in brackets (TN).]

Commentary

Being, spirit; Man or God; the mother unit of the Numbers, the first Substance. (El.L.)

Absolute being in the divine world.

Unity in the intellectual world.

Man in the psychic world.

The Counselor, the Principle, the Man, the Father, the Earth. (Pap.)

Divine unity. (Falc.).

Skill, cunning, diplomacy, dexterity. (J.B.)

General sense

Will.

CARD II - THE POPESS[1]

A woman crowned with a tiara, her head surrounded by a veil. She holds a book on her knees, which she hides with her cloak.

Astrological correspondence: The Moon.

Number: 2.

Letter: Bet ב. (P.P.)

COMMENTARY

The House of God and Man, the Sanctuary, the Gnosis, the Kabbalah, the Occult Church, the Binary, the Woman, the Mother. (El.L.)

The consciousness of the Absolute Being in the divine world.

The Binary of the Absolute Being in the intellectual world.

The Woman of the Absolute Being in the psychic world. (Chr.)

The counselor, the divine substance, the woman, the mother, the air. (Pap.)

Union of man and woman. (Falc.)

Secrets, mysteries. (J.B.)

GENERAL SENSE

Science.

---

1   In English this card's title usually is shown as *The High Priestess,* but its original name refers to a female Pope: a *Popess*; in French: *Le Papesse* (TN).

CARD III - THE EMPRESS

A winged woman, crowned and seated, holding at the end of her scepter the globe of the world. Her sign is an eagle, image of the soul and of life.

Astrological correspondence: Earth.

Letter: 3.

Letter: Ghimel ג. (P.P.)

COMMENTARY

The Word, the Ternary, fullness, fecundity, nature, generation. (El.L.)

The supreme and balanced power of active Intelligence and Wisdom: absolute in the divine world.

The universal Fecundity of Being in the intellectual world.

Nature acting in the physical world. (Chr.)

Action, initiative, divine nature, the Mercury of the Wise, generation, water. (Pap.)

Universal trinity: divine, spiritual and physical. (Falc.)

Germination, fertilization, generation, incubation, fermentation. (J.B.)

GENERAL SENSE

Action.

Card IV - The Emperor

A ruler whose body represents a right triangle and whose legs represent a cross, seated on a cubic throne.

Astrological correspondence: Jupiter.

Number: 4.

Letter: Dalet ד. (P.P)

Commentary

The gate or government in the East. The invitation, the power, the Tetragrammaton, the Cubical Stone. (El.L.)

The perpetual realization of the contained virtues of the Absolute Being in the divine world.

The realization of the Ideas of Contingent Being in the intellectual world.

Affirmation, negation, discussion, solution of the physical world. (Chr.)

Will, form, authority, protection, fire. (Pap.)

Unity completed by the trinity and giving the perfect square: affirmation, negation, discussion, solution. (Falc.)

Power, support, stability, a great character. (J.B.)

General sense

Realization.

CARD V - THE POPE

The Pope or great Hierophant, seated between the two columns of Hermes and Solomon. He makes the sign of esotericism and leans on the cross with three triangular crosspieces. In front of him, two lower ministers are kneeling.

Astrological correspondence: Mercury.

Number: 5.

Letter: He ה. (P.P.)

COMMENTARY

Indications, demonstration. Law, symbolism, religion, philosophy. (El.L.)

The new law regulating the infinite manifestations of Being in substance in the divine world.

Religion in the intellectual world.

Inspiration communicated with the astral fluid in the physical world. (Chr.)

Inspiration, universal magnetism, quintessence, religion. (Pap.)

Number 5, number of faith. (Falc.)

Inspiration, indication, man to whom appeal is made, priest, physician, lawyer. (J.B.)

GENERAL SENSE

Inspiration.

CARD VI - THE LOVER

A man between Vice and Virtue. Above him shines the Sun of Truth, and, in this Sun, Love, who stretches his bow and threatens Vice with his arrow.

Astrological correspondence: Virgo.

Number: 6.

Letter: Vav ٦. (P.P.)

COMMENTARY

Concatenation, hook, lingam, union, embrace, struggle, antagonism, combination. (El.L.)

The science of good and evil in the divine world.

Freedom and necessity in the intellectual world.

The antagonism of the natural forces in the physical world. (Chr.)

Love, Creation, Freedom. (Pap.)

Initiation through the test of Good and Evil, the balance between Heaven and Earth. (Falc.)

Attraction, love, beauty. (J.B.)

GENERAL SENSE

A test.

CARD VII - THE CHARIOT

A cubic four-columned chariot with a starry blue cloth. On the chariot, between the four columns, a crowned winner. He holds in his hand a scepter surmounted by a globe, a square and a triangle. His posture is haughty and calm; attached to the chariot are two sphinxes holding each other by the lower part, the belly; they pull one on one side and the other on the other; but one of them turns its head, so that both face the same side. On the chariot, and precisely at the front of it, is seen the Indian lingam crowned by the flying sphere of the Egyptians.

Astrological correspondence: Sagittarius.

Number: 7.

Letter: Zayin ז. (P.P.)

COMMENTARY

Weapons, triumph, sovereignty, priesthood. (El.L.)

The dominion of Spirit over nature in the divine world.

Priesthood and Empire in the intellectual world.

The subjection of the elements and matter to the intelligence in the physical world. (Chr.)

Triumph, victory, ability. (Pap.)

Providence, succor. (J.B.)

GENERAL SENSE

Victory.

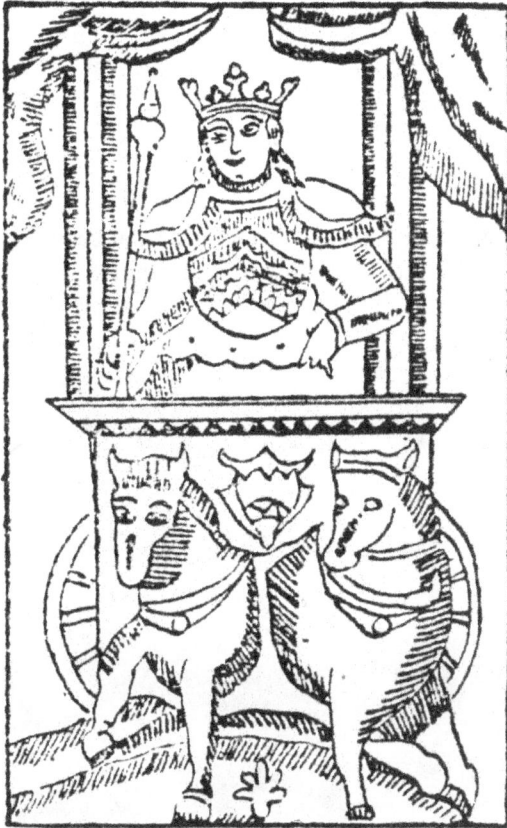

CARD VIII - JUSTICE

Justice with its sword and scales.

Astrological correspondence: Libra. (P.P.)

Number: 8.

Letter: Chet П.

COMMENTARY

Attraction and repulsion, life, fear, promise, threat. (El.L.)

Absolute justice in the divine world.

Attraction and repulsion in the intellectual world.

Relative justice, that of men in the physical world. (Chr.)

Justice. (Pap.) Number 8, that of justice and balanced reaction; harmony in the analogy of opposites. (Falc.) Justice, equity.

GENERAL SENSE

Equilibrium.

Card IX - The Hermit

A wise man leaning on a stick and holding a lamp in front of him. He wraps himself completely in his cloak.

Astrological correspondence: Neptune.

Number: 9.

Letter: Tet ט. (P.P.)

Commentary

Good, horror of evil, morality. (El.L.)

Absolute wisdom in the divine world.

Prudence in the intellectual world.

Circumspection in the physical world. (Chr.)

Prudence, protective genius, initiation. (Pap.)

The mirror image of the three worlds (3 x 3 = 9). (Falc.)

Prudence. (J.B.)

General sense

Prudence.

CARD X - WHEEL OF FORTUNE

A wheel in which a dog ascends on the right and a monkey descends on the left. At the top, a balancing sphinx holds a sword in its lion claws.

Astrological correspondence: Capricorn.

Number: 10.

Letter: Yod ׳.

COMMENTARY

Principle, manifestation, virile honor, phallus, virile fecundity, paternal scepter. (El.L.)

The active principle in the divine world.

The authority that governs the intellectual world.

Good or bad luck in the physical world. (Chr.)

Fortune, the kingdom of God, order. (Pap.)

The number 10, which contains all the others, is universal and absolute. The number of Being is 1, and that of non-Being 0.

Fortune, destiny, elevation. (J.B.)

GENERAL SENSE

Fortune.

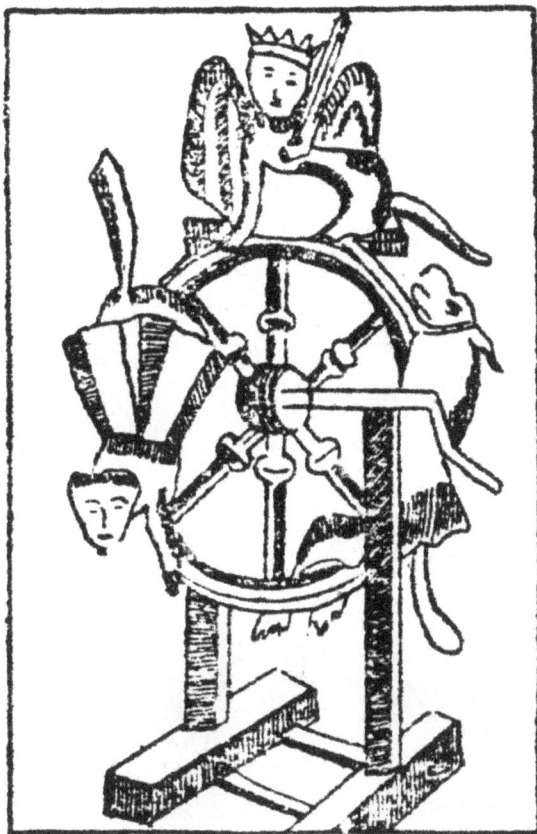

Card XI - Strength

A woman crowned with a vital ∞ and effortlessly closing the mouth of an enraged lion.

Astrological correspondence: Leo.

Number: 20.

Letter: Kaf כ. (P.P.)

Commentary

The hand in the act of taking and holding. (El.L.)

The Principle of all forces in the divine world.

Moral force in the intellectual world.

The organic force in the physical world. (Chr.)

Strength. (Pap.)

Force, energy, work. (J.B.)

General sense

Strength.

Card XII - The Hanged Man

A man hanging by one foot with his hands tied behind his back. His body forms a triangle with the point at the bottom and his legs a cross above the triangle. The gallows is in the shape of a Hebrew Tav (ת). The two trees supporting it have six branches cut off each.

Astrological correspondence: Uranus.

Number: 30.

Letter: Lamed ל. (P.P.)

Commentary

Example, teaching; public lecture. (El. L.)

The law revealed in the divine world.

The teaching of duty in the intellectual world.

The sacrifice in the physical world. (Chr.)

Judgment, sacrifice. (Pap.)

The man who dies for the Idea. (Falc.)

Atonement, sacrifice, martyrdom. (J.B.)

General sense

Sacrifice.

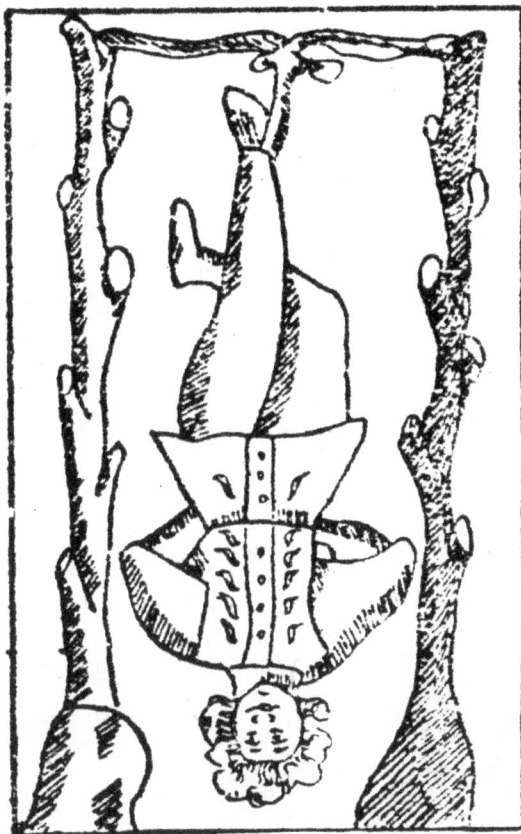

Card XIII - Death

Death reaping heads and hands in a meadow.
Astrological correspondence: Saturn.
Number: 40.
Letter: Mem מ. (P.P.)

Commentary

Domination and force, rebirth, creation, destruction. The sky of Jupiter and Mars. (El.L.)

The perpetual motion of creation, destruction and renewal in the divine world.

Ascension of the Spirit to the divine spheres in the intellectual world.

Natural death in the physical world. (Chr.)

Death, transmutation of forces. (Pap.).

Death. (J.B.)

General sense

Death.

CARD XIV - TEMPERANCE

An angel, who has the sign of the Sun on his forehead, pours from one vessel to another the two essences that compose the elixir of life.

Astrological correspondence: Aquarius.

Number: 50.

Letter: Nun ⴺ. (P.P.)

COMMENTARY

Sun's heaven, temperatures, seasons, change of life. (El.L.)

The perpetual motion of life in the divine world.

The combination of Ideas in the intellectual world.

The combination of Forces in the physical world. (Chr.).

Temperance, economy, reversibility, mixed harmony. (Pap.)

Metamorphosis, mutation. (J.B.)

GENERAL SENSE

Initiative.

CARD XV - THE DEVIL

The Goat of Mendes or the Baphomet of the Temple with his pantheistic attributes.

Astrological correspondence: Mars.

Number: 60.

Letter: Samech ס. (P.P.)

COMMENTARY

Mercury's heaven, occult science, magic, commerce, eloquence, mystery. (El.L.)

Predestination in the divine world.

Mystery in the intellectual world.

Fatality in the physical world. (Chr.)

Force majeure, disease, destiny, magic serpent. (Pap.)

The genius of evil, fatality and chaos. (Falc.)

Force majeure. (J.B.)

GENERAL SENSE

Fatality

CARD XVI - THE TOWER

A tower struck by lightning. Two people falling down it.
Astrological correspondence: Aries.
Number: 70.
Letter: Ayin **ע**. (P.P.)

COMMENTARY
Moon's heaven, disturbances, subversion. (El.L.)
The punishment of the Pride in the divine world.
The ruin of Spirit in the intellectual world.
The ruin of Fortune in the physical world. (Chr.)
Ruin. Broken material equilibrium. (Pap.)
Annihilation of pride and false science. (Fal.)
Fall, catastrophe. (J.B.)

GENERAL SENSE
Ruin.

Card XVII - The Star

A naked maiden pours upon a barren ground the fluids of Life flowing from two urns, one of gold and the other of silver. Above her head shines a Star of eight rays, surrounded by seven stars. Above a tree is a bird ready to take flight.

Astrological correspondence: Venus.

Number: 80.

Letter: Pe פ. (P.P.)

Commentary

Heaven of the soul. Effusion of thought, moral influence of the Idea on the Form. Immortality. (El.L.).

Immortality in the divine world.

Inner light in the intellectual world.

Hope in the physical world. (Chr.)

Hope. Divine natural forces. Nature. (Pap.)

Influence. Ascendancy. (J.B.)

General sense.

Hope.

CARD XVIII - THE MOON

The Moon, the dew, a crab about to come out of the water; two dogs barking at the Moon at the foot of two towers; a road disappearing on the horizon and strewn with drops of blood.

Astrological correspondence: Cancer.

Number: 90.

Letter: Tsadi **צ**. (P.P.)

COMMENTARY

The elements, the visible world, reflected light, material forms. (El.L.)

The abysses of the Infinite in the divine world.

The darkness of spirits subject to instincts in the intellectual world.

Delusions. Hidden enemies in the physical world. (Chr.)

Danger. Occult forces. Hidden enemies. (Pap.)

Darkness. Fright. (J.B.)

GENERAL SENSE.

Deception.

Card XIX - The Sun

A radiant Sun and two naked children holding hands in a fortified enclosure.

Astrological correspondence: Gemini.

Number: 100.

Letter: Qof ק. (P.P.)

Commentary

Blend, the head, the summit. (El.L.)

The Supreme Heaven in the divine world.

Sacred truth in the intellectual world.

Happiness in the physical world. (Chr.)

Material happiness. True light. Philosophical gold. (Pap.)

Light. Clarification. (J.B.)

General sense

Happiness.

Card XX - Judgment

A genie blows a trumpet. The dead come out of their graves; these reviving dead are a man, a woman and a child: the Ternary of human life.

Astrological correspondence: Pisces.

Number: 200.

Letter: Resh ר. (P. P.)

Commentary

The vegetative, the earth-generating virtue, eternal life. (El.L.)

Transition from earthly life to future life. (Chr.)

Change of position. Divine protection. Moral rebirth. (Pap.)

Awakening. Surprise. Splendor. (J.B.)

General sense

Renewal.

CARD XXI - THE WORLD

The kabbalistic crown between the four mysterious animals: the torn Sphinx. In the center the Truth holding a magic wand in each hand.

Astrological correspondence: Taurus.

Number: 400.

Letter: Shin 𐤔. (P.P.)

COMMENTARY

Microcosm. The summary of everything in everything. (El.L.)

State of the magician who has reached the highest degree of initiation. (Chr.)

A sure success. The absolute. Realization of the Great Work. Triumph. The Consultant. (J.B.)

GENERAL SENSE

The reward.

CARD 0 - THE FOOL

A man dressed as a jester, walks loaded with a saddlebag he carries behind him, full of his vices and ridiculousness; his disheveled clothes expose what they should hide. A dog, following him, bites him without him taking care to defend himself.

Astrological correspondence: Scorpio.

Number: 300.

Letter: Tav ת. (P.P.)

COMMENTARY

Seer. The flesh. Eternal life. (El.L.)

Man is the slave of matter. (Chr.)

Headache. Insanity. Interruption of divine communications. Moral blindness. Matter. (Pap.)

Unconsciousness. Aberration. Perturbation. Insanity. (J.B.)

GENERAL SENSE

Atonement.

Minor Arcana - II

Scepters

Ace of Scepters

A scepter[1] surmounted by an orb, in the midst of flames. Held by a hand. The hand evokes the idea of action and the realization of the will. The scepter is nothing more than an extension of the arm that acts or commands. This card thus represents the unity and the principle of action and power. It symbolizes the power conquered and attested by a fact or an object.

Elemental correspondence: Fire.

Meaning
Letter. Command. Edict. Decree.

---

1   Notice that Picard calls *Sceptres* (as the *Grand Belline* French Tarot deck) the suit that in most Tarot decks is called *Wands* (TN).

Two of Scepters

Two crossed scepters. At their base burns a moderate and invigorating fire that transforms humidity into vapor. In the center, ears of corn; at the top, bunches of grapes. This form symbolizes the union of two active forces called to combine for a high and moral objective.

The wheat and the vine, nourishing essences, indicate the practical and vital result of two forces associated for a productive end.

Meaning

Collaboration. Alliance.

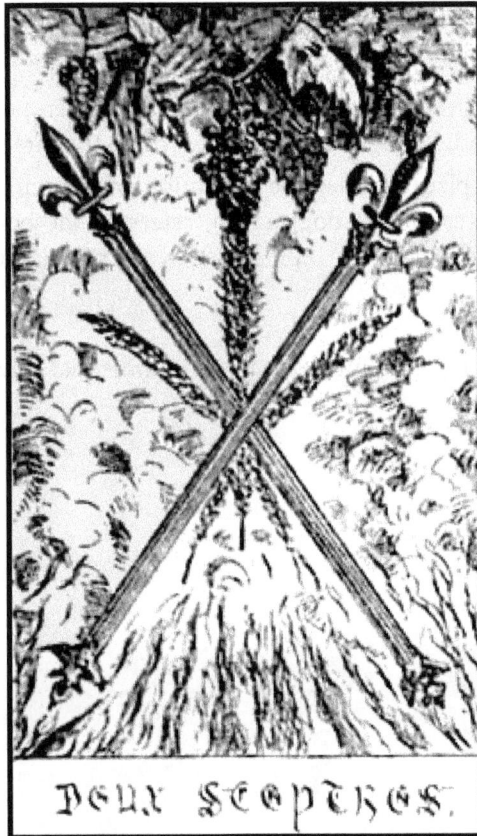

Deux Sceptres.

THREE OF SCEPTERS

Three scepters in the form of a triangle. In the center, a caduceus; at the top, a dog's head. Young hazel shoots surround the three scepters.

This arcanun, placed under the dominion of Mercury and recalling his attributes (caduceus, dog, hazel), refers to the beginning of the development of the activity represented by the previous arcanum.

MEANING

Beginning of success in intellectual and commercial enterprises.

Trois Sceptres.

FOUR OF SCEPTERS

Four scepters drawn in a square supported by a lion. In the center are ears of corn.

The quadrangular arrangement of the figure's details was adopted to emphasize the sense of achievement linked to the number 4 and its linear expression, the square. The lion represents the strength essential to achievement. It supports and protects. The ears of corn evoke the idea of fertility.

MEANING

Successful realization of intellectual conceptions.

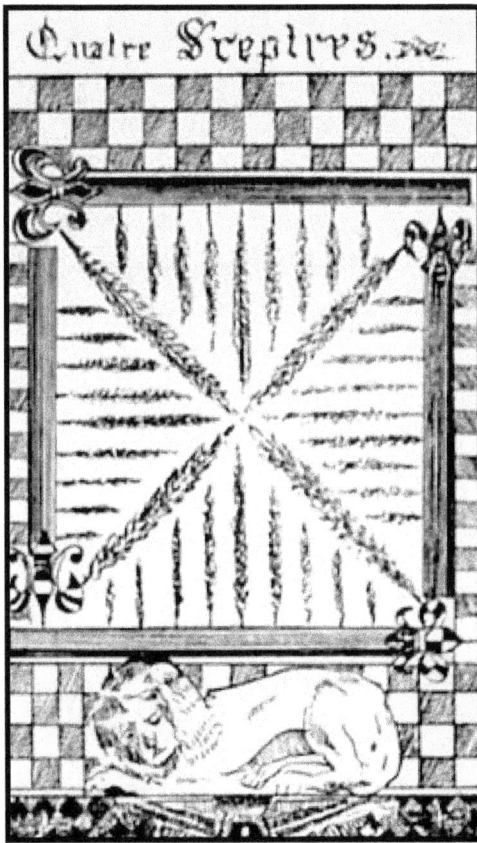

Five of Scepters

Five scepters forming a pentagram in the midst of flames.
It is the image of excessive moral activity.

Meaning
Ambition. Spirit of intrigue. Irritability. Anger. Alcohol.

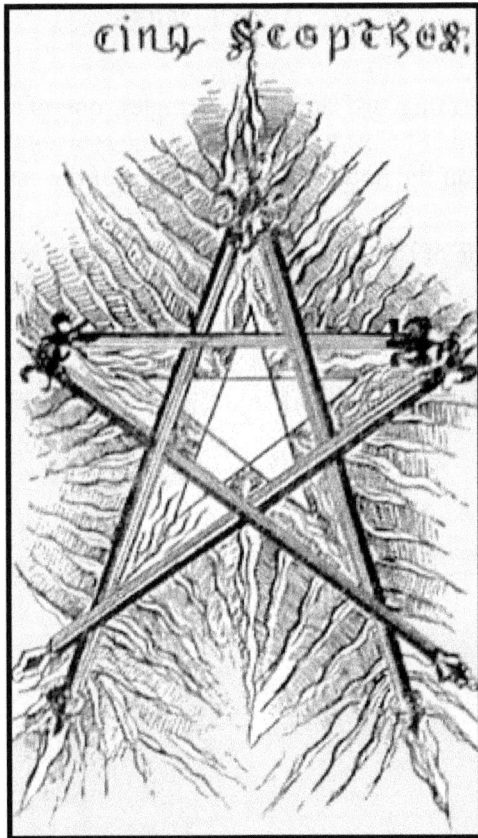

cinq Sceptres.

SIX OF SCEPTERS

Six scepters forming two opposing triangles, one of them above the earth and the other below it. Larvae gnaw the roots of the wheat, while the Sun rising on the horizon warms the tips of the ears, as if to make them ripen.

It is the struggle of two opposite active principles: the one that vivifies and the one that kills.

MEANING

Alternative of laziness and work in business.

SIX SCEPTRES

SEVEN OF SCEPTERS

Four scepters forming a square holding three scepters in a triangle. In the square, the heads of four animals corresponding to the four elements. In the triangle, the rising Sun.

The light that dominates the material world indicates the supremacy of the spirit over the elements.

MEANING
Invention.

EIGHT OF SCEPTERS

Eight scepters forming a star. The lower four scepters are surrounded by light flames that transform the atmosphere into vapors where the upper four scepters meet.

This is the image of the balance of the intellectual faculties. It is the genius disciplined by reason; it is also the temperate environment favorable to life; the zone of exchange.

MEANING

Balance. Commercial operations. Trees, grains and fruits. Among animals, mammals.

Huit Sceptres.

Huit. Sceptres.

Nine of Scepters

Four square scepters holding five scepters forming a pentagram. At the bottom, a lamp on which are engraved the signs of the fire trine. Above, flames surround the scepters.

This card expresses the prudence that must be brought to undertakings, as well as the clairvoyance of intelligence. It is suitable for very mature plans and projects. It implies duration. It corresponds to the slow development of ideas. The lamp recalls the attribute of the hermit in the 9th Major Arcana.

Meaning

Experience, acquisition of portable goods. Happy speculation in the stock market. Anything that suffers a delay or pause in action.

Ten of Scepters

Ten scepters surrounded by flames and arranged in a circle.

This card indicates an overabundance of activity and confers various gifts for multiple enterprises. It is especially applicable to works of the mind.

Meaning

Genius, scientific and encyclopedic works. By extension: scholars and artists. Harvest. Travel.

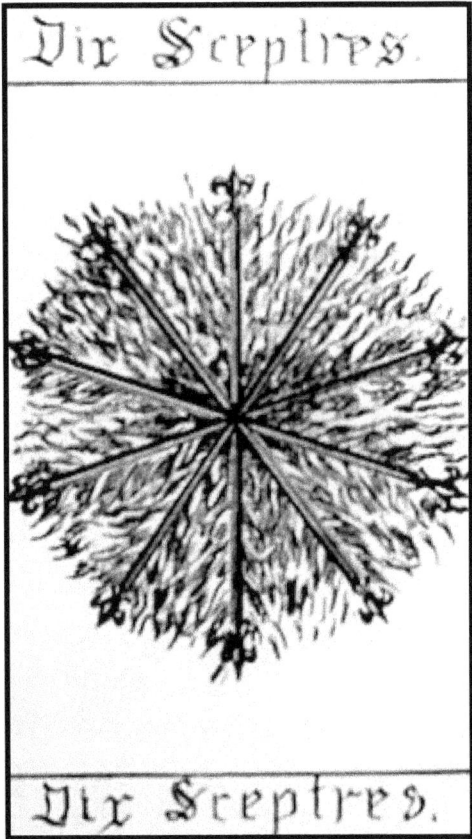

Dix Sceptres.

Dix Sceptres.

PAGE OF SCEPTERS

A kneeling page plants a scepter in the ground. To the right, fiery brands remind us the fire element.

The kneeling position indicates dependence in the hierarchical order of the human family and a dependence that applies to movement. In the ages of life, this card corresponds to the time when man is not fully adult. This last meaning remains fundamental to all the other pages and symbolizes adolescence (Age: 14 years).

MEANING

Postman. Domestics and, in general, adolescents who occupy secondary positions with respect to influential people.

Le Valet du Sceptre.

KNIGHT OF SCEPTERS

A knight on a galloping horse. He is riding towards the fire. On the right, the symbol of Aries, first sign of the fire trine. At the bottom, the helmet, an attribute of the knight, which is found in the other three knight cards.

This card applies to an adult, single man in an active position of a relatively higher order.

MEANING

Attaché of an embassy. Artists; famous actors. Inventors. Artists making their way in youth and chiefly men of letters. Scholars.

Le Chevalier du Sceptre.

QUEEN OF SCEPTERS

A queen holding a flaming scepter. She is standing on an arrow. The arrow symbolizes Sagittarius, the second fire sign. It is directed toward the Earth. The arcanum recalls the deeply educational character of Sagittarius as it applies to women.

MEANING

The educated, active and artistic woman. She may also be the wife of a scholar, a merchant or an artist.

La Reine du Sceptre.

KING OF SCEPTERS

A king standing on a lion, with a scepter in his hand. Behind him, a railing decorated with the attributes of the fire trine serves as a wall. Around him, flames rise into the air. This card represents the power acquired through work and activity. It is suitable for men who have risen through their own merit.

MEANING

Great inventors, merchants, artists and scholars. Men of genius.

Pentacles

ACE OF PENTACLES

A circular pentacle. Strong roots hold it to the earth. This arcanum symbolizes matter that is constrained by the earth element without being able to free itself from it.

Elemental correspondence: Earth.

MEANING

Money, considered in its broadest sense, that is, as a value representative of matter.

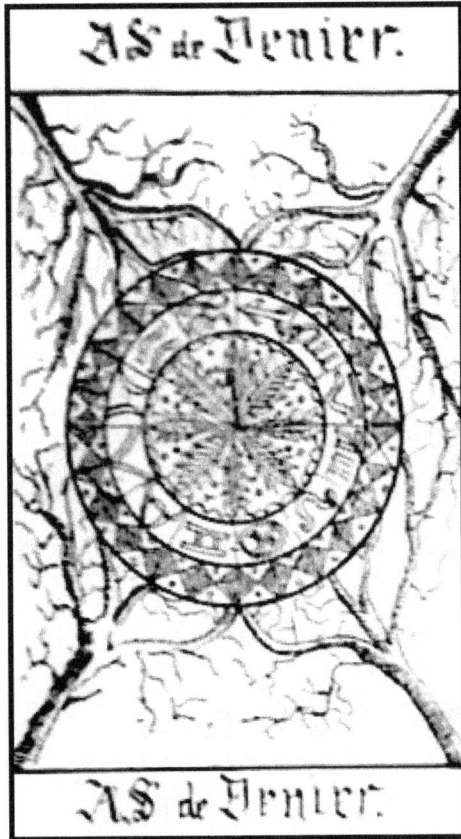

TWO OF PENTACLES

Two opposing pentacles. One of them, above the Earth and bearing the effigy of the Sun, is supported by two eagles; the other is held to the ground by roots. It bears the signs of the Earth and the Moon.

This arcanum symbolizes the antagonism of matter considered under two aspects: infra-terrestrial and supra-terrestrial matter; that is, the principle of absorption by gold and emancipation by gold; the law of exchange, of supply and demand.

MEANING

Commercial contract. Business partnership.

THREE OF PENTACLES

Two pentacles buried under the ground, while the third is placed on the ground as if it were the top of a triangle. In the earth: roots and a larva. On the pentacles are engraved the symbols of the terrestrial trine.

This card represents the beginning of the evolution of the idea in the service of the effort in all the enterprises that have as object the profit.

Taurus and Capricorn imply struggle, work. The larva about to emerge from the earth presages the transformation of matter into a certain product. In the soil, the roots reach out to release the third coin of the earthly embrace. Under the influence of Mercury, Virgo symbolizes the benefit of effort.

MEANING
Beginning of a business relationship.

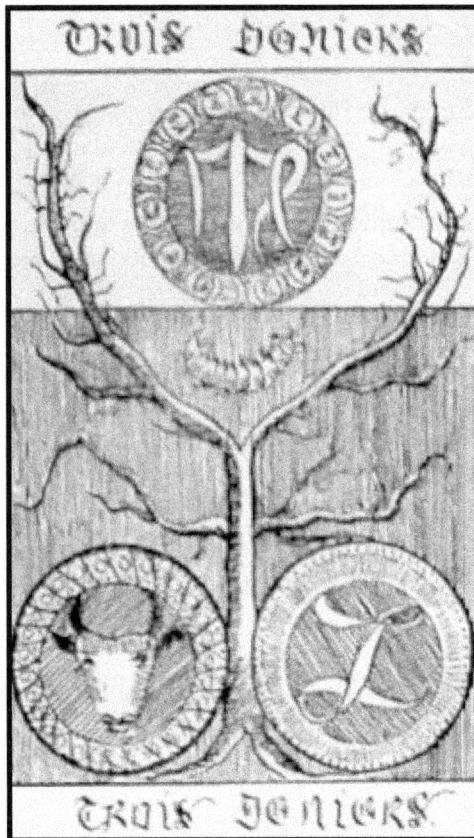

FOUR OF PENTACLES

Four pentacles in the middle of roots. In the center, the symbol of the Earth.

This card represents the realization of fortune. Its elemental correspondence with the Earth also attributes to it the birth of children and of animals that live under the earth, as well as reptiles.

MEANING

Fortune realized. Birth of a girl. Reptiles and animals that live under the earth. Cryptogams.

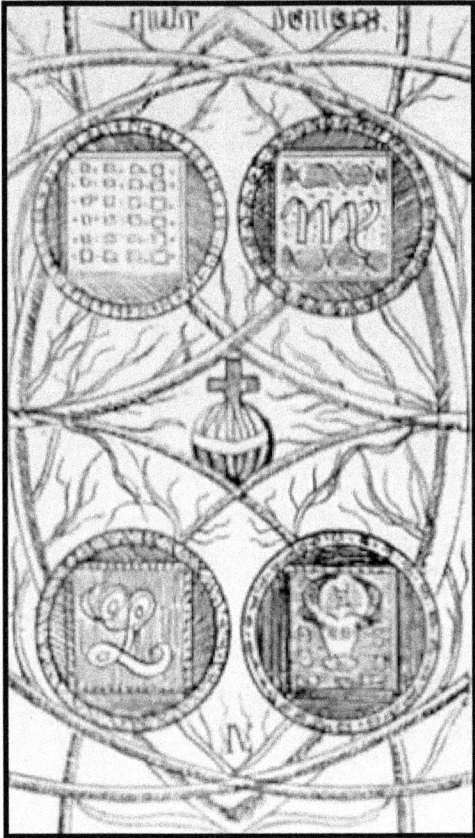

FIVE OF PENTACLES

Five pentacles around a pentagram. Flexible branches circulate between the pentacles. Five ants are engraved on the pentagram.

This card represents reason subduing fortune.

MEANING

Spirit of economy. Greed.

SIX OF PENTACLES

Six pentacles forming two opposing triangles, one of them above the earth and the other below the earth. On the three upper pentacles are engraved the symbols of the three theological virtues; on the lower ones, Capricorn's heads.

This card signifies that good and evil come into conflict for the good or bad use of fortune.

MEANING

Alternative of generosity or greed, or the good or bad use of money.

SEVEN OF PENTACLES

Four pentacles buried and arranged in a square. In the center, the Earth symbol is slightly blurred. On the ground, three pentacles form a triangle, a tree whose roots surround the four lower pentacles emerges from the ground. Its branches with young shoots run between the upper pentacles.

This card represents the moral force of money and its rational use.

MEANING

Benevolence.

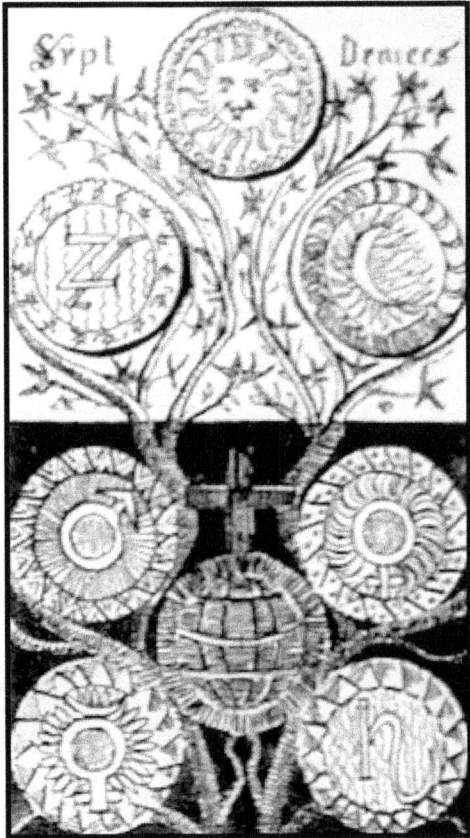

EIGHT OF PENTACLES

Eight pentacles placed between the rays of a star. Four pentacles are on the earth and the other four under the earth.

This card evokes the idea of equality in the distribution of goods and the fair distribution of wealth. It also corresponds to the age of reason for girls.

MEANING

Inheritance. A young girl. Minerals.

Huit Deniers.

Huit Deniers

NINE OF PENTACLES

Four pentacles in a square under the ground holding a pentagram between whose points are placed five pentacles surrounded by buds.

This card relates to reasoned and fruitful investments of money.

MEANING

Acquisition of land. Exploitation of mines. Grandmother.

TEN OF PENTACLES

Ten pentacles arranged in a circle. Half of them are under the earth; the other half, above the earth. In the earth, vegetation is active. It is the symbol of the evolution of matter.

This card indicates abundant gains and losses of money. It is the sign of fortune acquired in fortuitous and unstable circumstances.

MEANING

Luck as well as losses in gambling. Donations. The discovery of treasures.

Dix Deniers.

Page of Pentacles

A page standing on a pentacle rolling on dry ground; on either side, a bush with dead branches stands stiffly.

This card applies to young people who are ambitious for money without possessing the merits or faculties that secure wealth. They approach rich people without attaining wealth. They are recruited in the ordinary strata of society. Ill-disposed, this card indicates a propensity for theft.

Meaning
Servants. Thieves.

KNIGHT OF PENTACLES

A knight, bareheaded, guides his steed among the branches of trees covered with young leafs. Under the earth, the head of Taurus, first sign of the trine of the earth, surmounted by the helmet, attribute of the knight.

It is the symbol of the blind and ambitious man who relentlessly pursues his fortune through the trials of life. He wants to possess much and fast. In his career, his helmet fell off. His reason has no aegis. His inordinate ambition for money makes him lose all restraint. He is more active in circles where people play and have fun. For him, women are the main target. He considers her as the most remunerative income.

MEANING

Gamblers, croupiers, dowry seekers, exploiters of women. Theater directors.

Le Chevalier de Denier.

QUEEN OF PENTACLES

A queen haloed by a pentacle. She is standing and appears to be protected by a railing whose balusters form the symbol of Virgo, the second sign of the Earth trine.

This queen represents a woman who is able to secure a brilliant position. She is wealthy and derives her income from an irregular existence.

MEANING
The courtesan.

King of Pentacles

Seated on top of a rock, on a throne adorned with two Capricorn heads, a king holds in one hand a scepter crowned by the symbol of the Earth and in the other, a pentacle.

This card symbolizes the supreme power of gold, put into action by the ambitious. The steep rock indicates how hard the effort to reach fortune must have been. The bare summit reminds us of the earthly element in its most essential form. There is no vegetation to brighten the summit. Having reached the end of his hard race, the upstart is entitled to rest. He sits, isolated, like a dominator. Beneath his feet, he has sown desolation. Only gold is enough for him.

Meaning
The upstart.

Le ROI de DENIER

Cups

Ace of Cups

A cup with the symbols of the air signs: Gemini, Libra and Aquarius engraved on it. Eagles and butterflies complete the attributes of air. A castle rises from the cup. Above, a butterfly flies.

This arcanum represents the principle of love. From the bottom of the cup, where the passions are confusedly agitated, a synthesis emerges, strong and unbreakable; it is the family over which the butterfly hovers, symbol of the soul, as if to guarantee its immortality.

Elemental correspondence: Air.

Meaning
The family, the home.

As de Coupe.

TWO OF CUPS

Two cups in the middle of a wreath of roses.

This is the beneficial binary; the binary of the analogy relating to the loving principle. A cup with the active attributes of the Sun is on the same plane as another cup with the passive attributes of the Moon. The crown of roses – the flower of Venus – encloses them. It is the tendency of two loving principles of different nature to unite.

MEANING

Prospect of union, commitment and union if the neighboring arcana are favorable.

THREE OF CUPS

Three cups arranged in a triangle with an egg in the center. Above, a butterfly. The egg symbolizes the life of the seeds. The spring flowers represent the awakening of nature.

The beginning of the evolution of love, on the physiological level. The soul, in the figure of the butterfly, rises and clears above the physical plane.

MEANING

Pregnancy.

FOUR OF CUPS

Four cups drawn in a quadrilateral. In the center, an eaglet breaking its egg and coming out alive. Above, the sign of Gemini. On the sides, ears of corn and fruits.

This is the realization of life: birth. Gemini symbolizes childhood, ears of corn and fruits: fertility.

MEANING

Birth of male children or animals.

quatre coupes.

FIVE OF CUPS

Five cups placed on the sides of a pentagram. Around: birds, butterflies and flowers.

The idea of wisdom and will dominates in this card. It is the feeling that triumphs over the senses. The owl placed in the center of the pentagram presides over reflection and prudence in matters of love.

MEANING

Abnegation. Sacrifice. Discernment in the choice of friends. Renunciation of dangerous relationships.

SIX OF CUPS

Six cups forming two opposing triangles and surrounded by birds, butterflies and flowers.

The number 6 evokes the binary that presides over the division of the card into two equal parts, each containing 3 cups. These two divisions evoke at the same time the symbol of the 6th Major Arcanum (*The Lover*). This card thus expresses an idea of hesitation in matters of the heart.

MEANING

Torment, scruples before a decision to be made about a marriage.

SEVEN OF CUPS

Four cups in a square, dominated by three cups in a triangle. Around the cups, flowers in full bloom.

This card signifies victory in matters of love over material difficulties.

MEANING

Happy solution of material problems that hinder union plans.

Eight of Cups

Eight cups with butterfly wings symbolizing the air element are arranged in the shape of a star.

It is the balance of feelings and passion. The card also corresponds to the age of reason in men.

Meaning

Shared love. 7 years old children. All flying animals. Flowers.

NINE OF CUPS

Four cups in a square, supporting five cups in the shape of a pentagram. In the center of the four cups, a butterfly. Flowers around the cups.

This card expresses solicitude, the idea of love purified by time; attachment to the family.

MEANING

Respect for family traditions. Caring. The tradition of principles. Grandfather.

Neuf Coupes.

TEN OF CUPS

Ten cups arranged in a circle and separated by roses.

It is the perfect symbol of the most complex aspects of love and friendship. It is the set of all the affective faculties and their relationships between men.

MEANING

Friends.

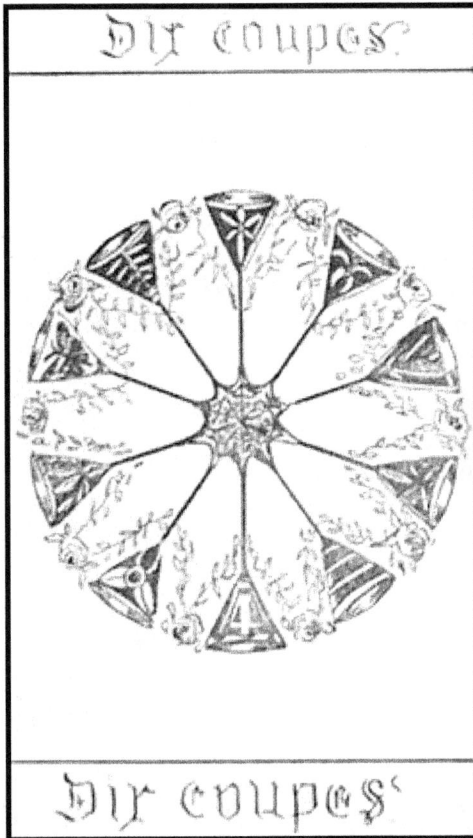

PAGE OF CUPS

A page kneels between two cups with flowers. He stretches out his hand towards a flower and breathes in its perfume.

This card represents the adolescent who feels the first emotions of love. It symbolizes the state of passivity towards women and also that kind of submission to which the inexperienced young man is subjected. It corresponds, therefore, to the phase of agitation and torment that marks the beginning of an affair. The butterfly indicates a propensity for sentimentality.

MEANING

Young man unhappy in love.

KNIGHT OF CUPS

A knight on a cup from which flowers are coming out. At the bottom, the helmet, attribute of the knight. At the top, the sign of Gemini, the first sign of the air trine.

This card symbolizes the idea of conquest and victory in love. It applies to the experienced and determined man who knows the resources of the charm that subjugates.

MEANING
The seducer.

QUEEN OF CUPS

A queen standing holding a cup over which flies a butterfly. In the background, a cup held by two eagles. The sign of Libra, the second sign of the air trine, is placed in front of the cup.

This card represents an accomplished woman. It characterizes the perfect wife, loving and kind, of high rank, wealthy and a good mother.

MEANING
The wife, the mother.

La Reine de Coupe.

KING OF CUPS

A standing king holds in one hand a pickax turned toward the ground and in the other a scepter topped by a butterfly. In front of him is a cup placed on a pedestal. Four streams of water come out of the cup, forming the sign of Aquarius and fertilizing the earth.

Intelligence and will, symbolized by the scepter, must be at the service of effort – the pickax – to fertilize any enterprise. The luck that comes from above is only ephemeral or sterile if it does not find a counterpart of guarantee represented by work, which nourishes it and gives it stability.

MEANING
The husband. The father of the family.

Le Rui de Coupe.

Swords

ACE OF SWORDS

A sword held by a hand in still water. Its point pierces a crayfish. In the sky, the crescent moon.

This card represents the beginning of a fight. The arm, the organ of action, holds the sword to signify that force must be directed by the will. The attributes of the Moon: the water and the crayfish evoke the nature of the invisible difficulties of the obstacles to overcome.

Elemental correspondence: Water.

MEANING
Fight.

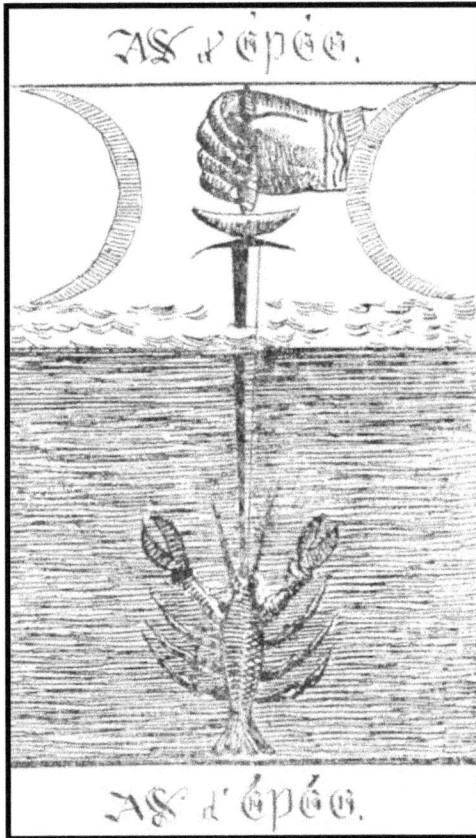

TWO OF SWORDS

Two swords with their opposing points. One touches the sky, the other plunges into a raging sea.

This card symbolizes the antagonism of two opposing forces that are represented by the two opposing elements, water and fire, which act here through the extreme manifestations: the storm and the lightning.

MEANING
Rupture. Duel.

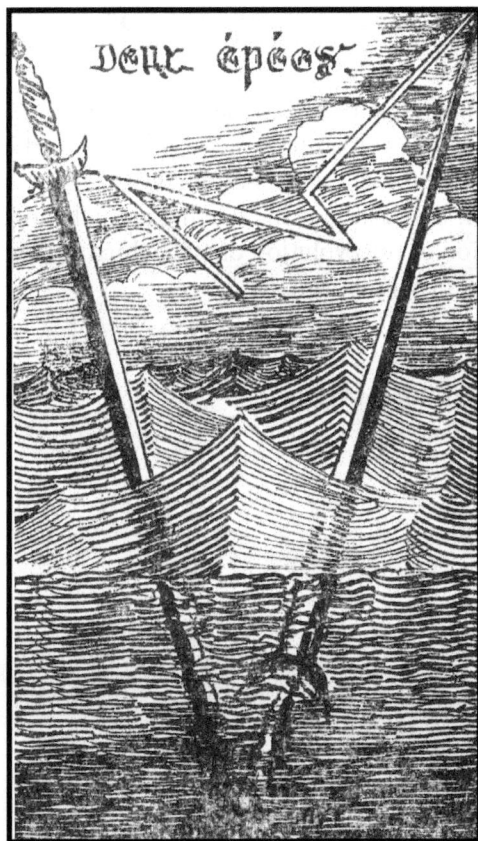

Three of Swords

Three swords forming a triangle. They are in murky water. The tips of the two side swords push an upturned fish to the surface. Three water lily leafs, hit by the tips, fall to the bottom dying. The position of the fish with its belly on the surface is the one the animal adopts when it dies. This is the period of the evolution of evil, which makes its first attacks against any vital or moral principle.

Meaning
Perverse instincts. Morbid state.

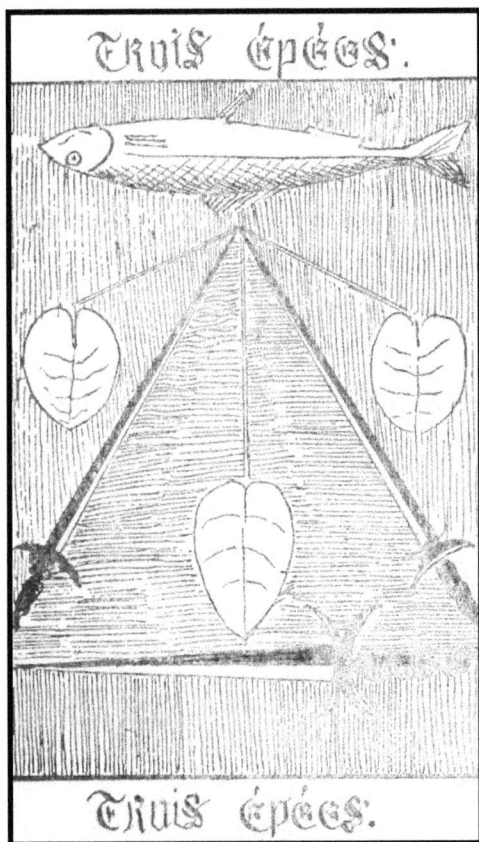

Trois épées.

Trois épées.

FOUR OF SWORDS

Four swords whose points converge towards a central point in the middle of the water. Around the points, the sign of Scorpio. The water is bounded by quarter Moons. At the top, the sign of Cancer. The power of the points, well known in magic, is exerted here on Scorpio, an evil water sign. It is the realization of evil on all planes, especially on the physical plane.

MEANING
Disease declared. Attack.

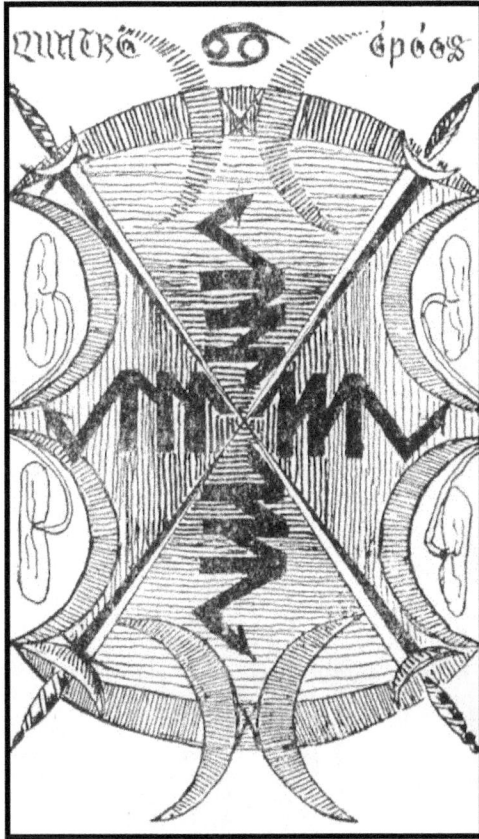

FIVE OF SWORDS

Five swords forming a pentagram in a rough sea. At the top, the eye of God.

This card refers to the reflex effect of evil on the perpetrator. The eye of God opening in the serenity of heaven evokes the idea of the supremacy of conscience.

MEANING

Remorse, moral punishment, the cry of conscience.

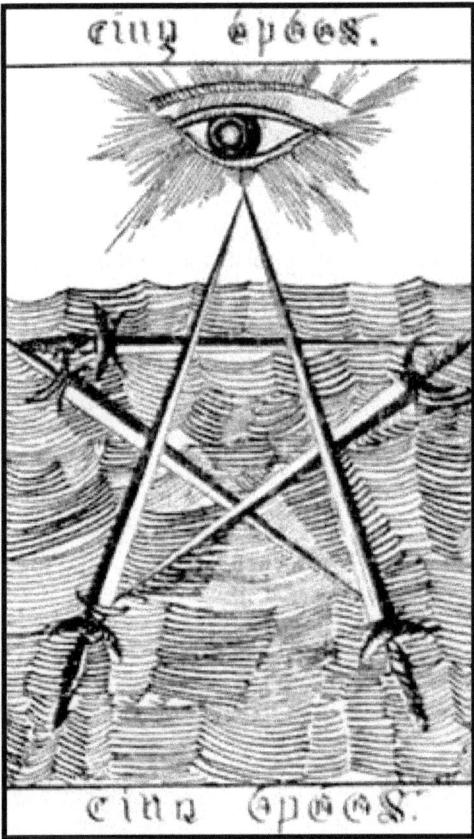

SIX OF SWORDS

Six swords forming two opposing triangles, one of which has its lower point under water, while the other one has its vertex in the air.

At the bottom of the water, a crayfish; in the air, two ram's heads.

The heads of the animals are reminiscent of two of signs the of the zodiac: Cancer and Aries, of opposite elemental nature (fire and water). It is the symbol of the struggle between emancipation and servitude, between freedom and necessity.

MEANING
Dependence. Undecided state of health.

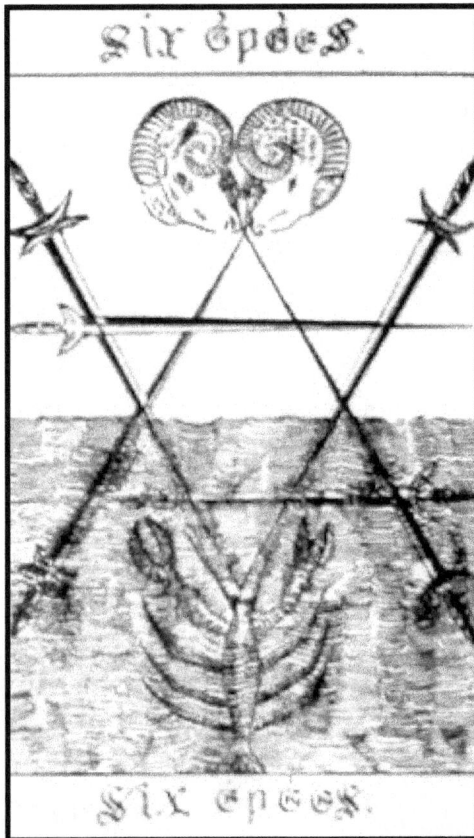

Seven of Swords

Four swords in the shape of a square, placed in the water, hold three other swords in a triangle at water level. The cold Moon, mistress of the nights, shines over the Sun, which sinks into the depths of the water. This is the supremacy of darkness over light.

This arcanum applies to evil deeds, to the temporary success of the wicked, to shady undertakings.

Meaning

Armed robbery. Betrayal.

EIGHT OF SWORDS

Eight swords arranged in the form of a star; four swords are in the water and four in the air. The number 8 evokes the idea of balance and justice. This card expresses the sanctions of Justice.

MEANING

Condemnation. The fish. Water plants.

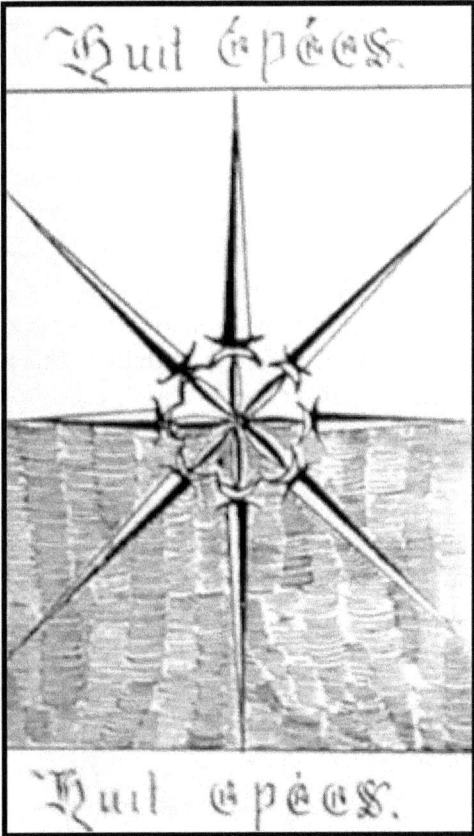

Huit épées.

Huit épées.

NINE OF SWORDS

Four swords in a square at the bottom of the water hold five swords in the air forming a pentagram, surrounded by water lily leafs. Two fish, with their heads turned toward the surface of the water, seem to want to jump out of their element. It represents the attraction exerted by the spirit of evil (V) which temporarily prevails over its realization (IV).

This card applies to the revenge planned in seclusion and matured by patience. It also expresses feelings of hatred and envy. It summarizes what evil expresses on the plane of concentration. It therefore marks the pause between intention and act.

MEANING

Hate. Envy. Affections that undermine the organism in an attenuated form and that do not manifest themselves in an acute state. Intoxication. Alcoholism. State of decrepitude.

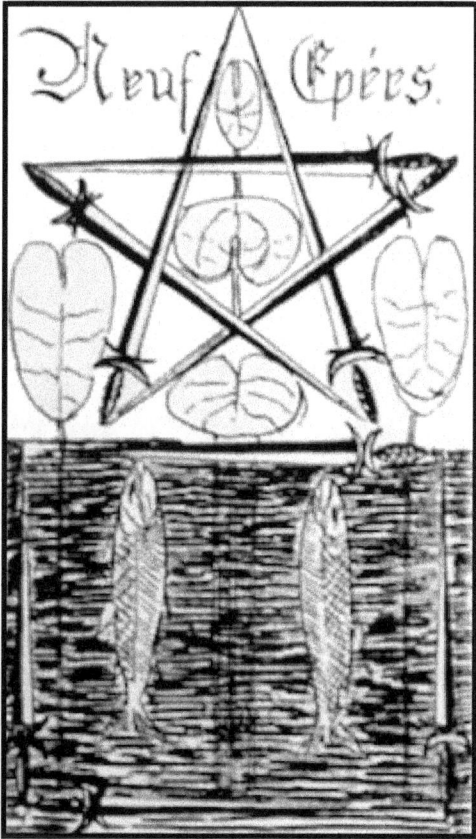

TEN OF SWORDS

Ten swords arranged in a circle. Half of them are in the water; the other half in the air. In the four corners of the figure, the Moon in its four phases, to signify the mobility of the evolution of evil.

This card represents the extreme variety of forms of evil as well as all the threats hanging over our heads.

MEANING
Enemies. Epidemic or contagious diseases.

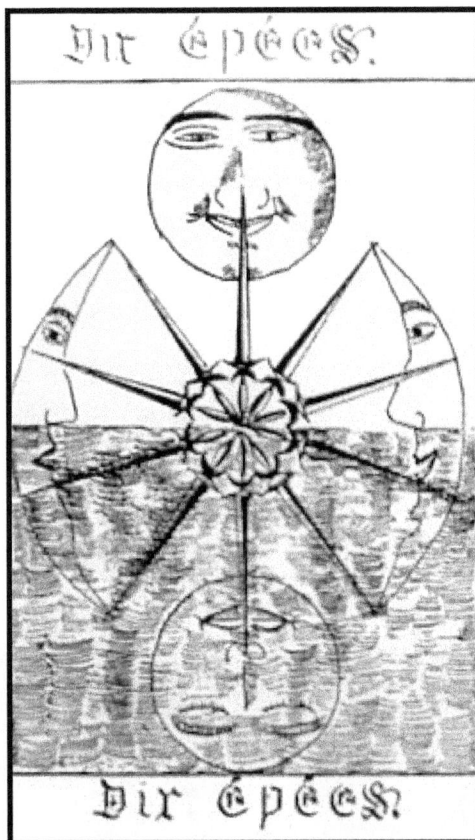

PAGE OF SWORDS

A page of lofty stature holding a sword. He stands on a checkerboard floor, at the water's edge, in the attitude of one who spies. The checkerboard signifies that the plan in which the page moves involves skillful combinations. He appears to be waiting, ready to attack.

MEANING
Night prowlers. Soldier.

Knight of Swords

A knight whose steed is swimming in the water. Above, the helmet, attribute of the knight, and the Scorpion.

This card applies to subordinates, to fearless people who rush headlong into battle, to political or religious fanatics. It implies an activity carried out for an essentially practical purpose and through the use of brute force.

Meaning

Adventurers. Religious fanatics. Non-commissioned officers. Bailiffs. Lawyers. Sportsmen. Popular speakers. Thugs.

Le Chevalier d'Epée.

QUEEN OF SWORDS

A queen, standing on a crescent moon sailing over the surface of the waters in the form of a gondola. She holds a sword. In the sky, the sign of Cancer.

The aquatic element is represented here by its most powerful attributes: the Moon, the Sea, Cancer; moreover, it is personified by the woman.

This card symbolizes the woman with a fertile imagination, who pursues several projects at once. Difficulties do not discourage her. She is armed for battle and does not shy away from any means to achieve her ends.

MEANING

A conspirator. A widow.

King of Swords

On a broad river of majestic course, sails a king, standing on the crescent moon. His sword touches two fish. The river, Pisces, and the king's noble bearing correspond to the influences of Jupiter. This king shares the prerogatives of magistrates, generals and ecclesiastics.

Meaning

The officials. The priests. Magistrates. Widowers.

Le Roi d'Epée.

Interpretation

Not everyone can become capable of manipulating the Tarot; or, as they say in the vernacular, be able to read the cards. It is not enough to know the cards perfectly. Science without intuition is like a body without a soul. To be able to read the cards well, one must have the mysterious gift of clairvoyance that puts us in relation with the astral plane. Rare are the privileged ones who possess this faculty; sometimes they themselves are not aware of it. If chance or circumstances induce them to use the Tarot, they are attracted, fascinated, so to speak, by the symbols. They assimilate the elements of their correspondence with prodigious rapidity, and are never shocked by the ambiguous meaning of certain cards. They speak fluently; they impose themselves by the clarity of their assumption; they see. Do not ask them why or how they have seen. They know nothing. They are mere agents of an ultra-earthly truth which they can contemplate without effort and translate without freedom. However, one must not conclude from this that their predictions are the fruit of imagination. They respect the principles; they know them; but their power as seers transports them so quickly into the astral that they suddenly grasp the deductions. Whatever their talents may be, they develop their gifts by practice, and always associate a certain amount of effort with their natural lights. It would be detrimental to the dignity of the Tarot to suppose that, being carried away by fits of imagination, one can call oneself a seer. When it comes to true clairvoyants, there is an irrefutable proof: the making of predictions. Therefore, there is no clairvoyance without realization.

Below these rare privileged categories, there are beings more or less willing to enter the currents of light and truth. To attain a higher clairvoyance, they must prepare themselves, through the methodical practice of the Tarot, for the education of the gifts they possess in germ. Finally, there are many people who, in spite of all their good will and application, will never become capable of reading the cards.

How can one know the degree of ability one naturally possesses? It is very simple, and the explanation of the answer sought will immediately give us the opportunity to state the general rules governing divination by means of the Tarot.

One interprets the cards for oneself or for another person. It is best to isolate oneself as much as possible or to remain only in the presence of the querent. One faces the operation in a state of mind free of any idea of personal interest or ill-conceived curiosity. It is necessary to have a great mental elasticity, not to make any effort of imagination that could alter the particular freshness of the intuition. It is necessary as well to be fasting, in a very clean room, and to avoid noise and any violent movement of lights, in a word anything that can distract or disturb. Once this has been achieved, one must abstract oneself in the thought of an accomplished work or of a past thing. It is an operation of control destined to enlighten the operator and to confirm him if he is in the necessary disposition to question the future. One always has the certainty of what happened the same day. For example, the common case of receiving a missive. Therefore, think well about the card you received and, before taking 4 cards (this time from the Tarot deck), remember that the cards are symbolized by the ace, the page, or the knight of scepters, or, more generally, by any card of scepters, which indicate movement. Turn over the 4 cards. If in these 4 cards you find a symbol corresponding to the missive received, you can be sure that you are in a state conducive to divination. Because you should never lose sight of the fact that you are not always in the right state of mind. In such a case, do not strive, do not persist, leave the experience for another day.

If the check carried out is satisfactory, 16 cards will be taken. We chose this number because it is the square of 4 and, as 4 is the number of realization, we believe that, repeated by itself, it will be the most complete expression of the desired realization of the things of the future. We do not attribute any card to the querent, for a very simple reason: if the querent is present, it is useless for him to be represented. Moreover, by attributing to a card the correspondence of the querent, we suppress the true meaning of the card itself. This substitution would actually deprive us of an arcanum.

The distribution of the cards is observed by first distinguishing the domain of the major and minor arcana; then that of the symbols. When the major arcana dominate, the events are distant; if the minor arcana dominate, the opposite occurs; for we have said that the cycle of the Major Arcana conforms to the causes and that of the Minor Arcana to the immediate effects.

If the cards are reversed, they do not change their meaning at all; but their effect will be less intense. The inverted position seems to correspond to the astrological nobility of retrogradation. The meaning of each card is then interpreted according to its meaning in the reading from right to left. The surest way to avoid getting lost in a fantastic translation of the arcana is to assign to them their main meaning, without discarding too much. In this way a literal summary of the meaning of the symbols will be obtained, striving to see the spirit behind the letter. After this general analysis, the 16 cards are taken, shuffled and placed again in 4 piles of 4 cards each.

Here we find the elementary Quaternary and its correspondences.

The first pile will inform us of what is related to Fire, action; the second will be that of Earth, wealth; the third, that of Air, love; the fourth, that of Water, struggle.

* * *

There are other excellent methods for interpreting the cards among which we especially recommend that of the Gypsies, recommended by Bourgeat. This method confirms the relationship of the Tarot with astrology, and the arrangement of the cards indicates is nothing other than the representation of an astrological scheme considered under the aspect of the dominations.

Twelve piles of 4 cards each are arranged in the form of a circle. Each group represents a house of the horoscope with the meaning attributed to it by Tradition and which we recall.

The first pile represents the subject, his health, his physique; the second, possessions; the third, his siblings; the fourth, his father; the fifth, his children; the sixth, sickness; the seventh, marriage; the eighth, death, inheritance; the ninth, travel, religion; the tenth, status, honors; the eleventh, friends; the twelfth, enemies.

Going deeper into the domain of astrology, one could apply this method not only to the study of each house, but also to the relationships of the houses to each other and establish from this a system of prognostication based on their aspects. But we think it prudent never to recommend the more complicated method.

One can arrange the charts in various ways. When one reads about different methods, it is natural to wonder whether the adoption of too many procedures will not sow some confusion in the spirit. A book can only be read in one way, but it can be commented on in many ways. The same is true of the Tarot. One will work wisely by developing it as simply as possible. The difficulty will be in the interpretation.

It remains for us to recommend a practical and very simple method to obtain an answer to the question posed. One concentrates on the question and takes four cards that should provide the elements of realization. It is not very rare to observe with practice that, repeating the same question over and over again, one takes several times in succession the same four cards that give the answer.

It may be objected that we have presented methods of interpretation without supporting them with examples. We have done so on purpose. Interpretation is an art. It requires a special tact of which no treatise can give an idea. In general, the examples extracted from Tarot books have an obligatory character. This is understood. The authors have tried to approximate the arcana whose meaning is completed, no doubt, to clarify the difficulties. In practice, it is not the same. The most opposite arcana and symbols often meet side by side, so it is necessary to reconcile their meanings. This work belongs to the operator, and cannot be planned or organized in advance. On the other hand, throughout this book we have tried to emphasize to the reader the importance of other factors, such as initiative, will and personal effort. We could not end in a better way than by emphasizing their importance.

Bibliography

Pierre Piobb	*Formulaire de Haute Magie*	P.P.
Éliphas Lévi	*Dogme et rituel de la haute magie*	El.L.
Paul Christian	*Histoire de la Magie*	Chr.
Papus	*Le Tarot Divinatoire*	Pap.
R. Falconnier	*Les XXII lames hermétiques du tarot divinatoire*	Falc.
J. G. Bourgeat	*Le Tarot*	J.B.

www.ingramcontent.com/pod-product-compliance
Lightning Source LLC
Chambersburg PA
CBHW072140090426
42739CB00013B/3231